Symbols of Power
Masterpieces from the Nanjing Museum

CURATOR
Xu Huping

CONSULTING CURATOR
Lydia Thompson, Ph.D.

The Bowers Museum of Cultural Art
Santa Ana, California in association with
The Nanjing Museum, Nanjing, China

BOWERS MUSEUM

copyright © 2002 Bowers Museum of Cultural Art
All rights reserved

Design: Barney Wan with Ian Roberts, London, UK

Catalogue editing and translation:
Vickie C. Byrd, I-Huey Chu, and Nancy Ravenhall Johnson

ISBN: 0-9679612-3-8

Exhibition organized by:
The Bowers Museum of Cultural Art, Santa Ana, California, and
The Nanjing Museum, Nanjing, China

Major Funding for this exhibition was provided by:
Los Angeles Times, D. Diane Anderson, Janice and Ted Smith, Boeing North American, Inc.
Fletcher Jones Foundation, The First American Corporation, and Resources Connection

Additional funding was provided by:
S. L. and Betty Huang, Albert and Lia Wang, J. Bicknell and Mary Ann Lockhart
Aminco International (USA), Inc., Cathay Bank, and Salvatore Ferragamo

Special thanks also goes to:
United, South Coast Plaza, and Noelle Corporate Communications

Exhibition schedule for
Symbols of Power: Masterpieces from the Nanjing Museum
The Bowers Museum of Cultural Art
June 9, 2002-May 4, 2003
2002 North Main St.
Santa Ana, CA 92706
Telephone: 714 567 3600
www.bowers.org

Printed and bound in Taiwan by Choice Lithographers

Contents

Preface

Foreword

Chronology of China's History

Introduction

Symbols of Power in the Tomb

Symbols of Power in the Temple

Symbols of Power at Court

Symbols of Power beyond the Court

Sponsor's Statement

Resources Connection is proud to support The Bowers Museum exhibit Symbols of Power: Masterpieces from the Nanjing Museum. Partnering with the Bowers has allowed us over the years to be part of an effort of bringing world-class exhibits to Orange County.

Since many of these objects have not been shown even in China, this exhibit provides a rare opportunity for those in our community to glimpse the rich history of beauty, culture, and tradition as shown through Chinese symbolism.

It is a pleasure and a privilege to support a truly unique and spectacular exhibit such as this. We wish to thank professor Xu Huping and the Nanjing Museum for allowing these ancient treasures to be viewed in the United States.

Donald B. Murray,
Chairman and Chief Executive Officer,
Resources Connection LLC

Preface

China and America are two great countries. Even though there are many cultural and traditional differences between them, the people of both nations fought side by side during World War II, thus establishing a valuable, profound friendship.

And now, two great cultural institutions, the Nanjing Museum and the Bowers Museum of Cultural Art, are jointly presenting the exhibit Symbols of Power: Masterpieces from the Nanjing Museum. This partnership doubtlessly makes our friendship stronger.

The Nanjing Museum, formally called the National Central Museum and founded in 1933, was the first multi-functional museum established in China. It was the first Chinese museum to adapt scientific methods to collect, preserve, conserve, and study historic objects. During the past 70 years, both the quality and quantity of the Nanjing Museum's collection have grown into a remarkable achievement.

As a world-renowned museum, the Nanjing Museum has a collection of more than 400,000 Chinese objects. The collection came from three sources. The first was excavations by museum staff in the early and middle 20th century; these objects are of great value in history, art, and science, and include pottery, stoneware, and jade from the Neolithic period, bronze vessels from the Shang and Zhou dynasties, light blue porcelain from the Six Dynasties, and gold, silver, jade, porcelain, and other forms of artwork from the Sui, Tang, Song, Yuan, Ming, and Qing dynasties. The second source was imperial objects collected by the royal family and passed down, generation by generation, in the imperial palace. These include porcelain produced by the imperial kiln, calligraphy, paintings, and handicrafts. The third source was private collectors, who donated jades and bronze from the Shang and Zhou dynasties, pottery and porcelain from the Han and Six Dynasties, and paintings, jades, sculptures, stone tablets, and inscriptions from the Ming and Qing dynasties. These national treasures reflect the splendor and diversity of Chinese history. Nanjing was the capital of many dynasties, and the richness of these collections indicates the economic, political, and cultural movement towards the south of China.

The Bowers Museum of Cultural Art is one of the most outstanding museums in Southern California. Since its reopening in 1992, under the leadership of Dr. Peter Keller and with the dedication of Mrs. Anne Shih of the Board of Governors, the Bowers Museum has hosted many exhibitions of Chinese culture. Its hard work and contributions to promoting cultural exchange have moved and benefited many people. The Nanjing Museum is very proud to have the opportunity to work with the Bowers Museum to present this wonderful exhibit to further the understanding and appreciation of Chinese culture, tradition, art, and history among American people and generations of Chinese people who live in the United States. We truly believe that this exhibit will enhance the trust and strengthen the friendship between America and China.

Xu Huping
Director
The Nanjing Museum

Pottery Bowl Painted with Floral Design
Neolithic period, Dawenkou culture (c. 5000-2250 BC)
Height: 9.6 cm; Diameter: 14.3 cm
Excavated at Dadunzi, Pizhou, Jiangsu province, in 1976

Made of fine red clay, the upper part of the vessel was first coated in white and then painted with triangles formed by curved lines in red, so that the remaining areas in white resemble connected cruciform flower petals. The veins and pistils are painted in dark brown.

Foreword

On the heels of the Bowers Museum's widely acclaimed national tour of *Secret world of the Forbidden City: Splendors from China's Imperial Palace* exhibition, co-organized with the Palace Museum, Beijing, we are very proud to be be presenting *Symbols of Power: Masterpieces from the Nanjing Museum*. This exhibit is the second in what promises to be a very exciting series of exhibitions highlighting China's rich history. *Symbols of Power: Masterpieces from the Nanjing Museum* is quite different, and in many ways more exciting than our *Secret world of the Forbidden City* exhibition. *Secret world* brought us magnificent treasures from a relatively short, but rich period of China's history; from 1644 to 1911. *Symbols of Power* includes many imperial treasures from this same span of time, but goes way beyond and includes very important pieces that in one way or another symbolise the power of the Emperor and his court over 5,000 years of Chinese history. Certainly many of the pieces are considered national treasures and are being seen for the first time outside of China.

During the course of organizing *Symbols of Power* we have come to know the Nanjing Museum, its Director, Dr. Xu Huping, and his staff. The relationship that has developed between our two institutions is as rare as the objects we are bringing to the United States from his storerooms and exhibit galleries. The Nanjing Museum was the national Museum of China for many years, and its collections reflect its status. Director Xu and his staff opened the doors to all his storerooms to assure the finest exhibition possible and the quality of this exhibition reflects his tremendous effort. Many of the objects were once part of a heroic effort in the 1930s and 40s to save their rich Chinese heritage from an invading Japanese army. Many objects were only recently unpacked from their crude shipping crates. Other treasures are recent discoveries from ongoing archeological excavations in and around Jiangsu province. Some of these recent discoveries are so important that they too are classified as "national treasures". However, it must be emphasised that without the close personal relationship that has developed between the Bowers and Nanjing Museums, this exhibition would have been impossible to produce.

No exhibition of the magnitude of *Symbols of Power* is possible without the aid of of many talented and dedicated individuals. In addition to Mr. Xu and the staff of the Nanjing Museum, there are many individuals who must be acknowledged here in the United States. First and foremost is Mrs. Anne Shih. A member of the Bowers Museum's Board of Governors and a tireless proponent of Chinese history and culture, Mrs. Shih has done more to facilitate this exhibition than anyone can possibly imagine. She is the ultimate "culture broker". Our cultural consultant, Dr. Lydia Thompson, has done a superb job in organizing all the academic aspects of this exhibition. Her colleague, Audrey Spiro, reviewed much of Dr. Thompson's work. The exhibit's staff headed up by Paul Johnson did an amazing job in the presentation of the exhibition, and Nancy Johnson should be recognized for her incredible graphics that are presented throughout the exhibition. Anne Bennett and Alice Bryant worked tirelessly in condition-reporting the exhibition and I-Huey Chu spent literally hundreds of hours translating texts and facilitating all aspects of our communications with Nanjing. Finally, Barney Wan must be acknowledged for his creative work in designing this catalogue.

Peter C. Keller, Ph.D.

Chronology

The objects in this exhibition date from *c.* 5000 BC to the present day.

Late Neolithic period	*c.* 5000-2000 BC
Yangshao Culture (Henan, Shaanxi)	*c.* 5000-2750 BC
Majiayao Culture (Gansu, Qinghai)	*c.* 4000-2250 BC
Dawenkou Culture (Shandong, Jiangsu)	*c.* 5000-2250 BC
Hongshan Culture	*c.* 4500-2750 BC
Liangzhu Culture (Jiangsu, Shanghai, Zhejiang)	*c.* 3300-2250 BC
Longshan Culture (Shandong)	*c.* 3000-1700 BC
Xia dynasty	*c.* 2000-1600 BC
Shang dynasty	*c.* 1500-*c.* 1050 BC
Zhou dynasty	*c.* 1050-256 BC
Western Zhou	*c.* 1050-771 BC
Eastern Zhou	*c.* 770-256 BC
Spring and Autumn period	*c.* 770-450 BC
Warring States period	*c.* 450-221 BC
Qin dynasty	221-206 BC
Han dynasty	206 BC-220
Western Han	206 BC-9
Usurpation of Wang Mang	9-23
Eastern Han	25-220
Period of Division	220-581
Three Kingdoms	220-265
Wei	220-280
Shu	221-263
Wu	222-280
Western Jin dynasty	265-316
Eastern Jin dynasty	317-420
Southern dynasties	
Liu Song	420-479
Southern Qi	479-502
Liang	502-557
Chen	557-589
Northern dynasties	
Northern Wei (Tagbatch/Tuoba)	386-534
Eastern Wei	534-549
Western Wei	535-556
Northern Qi	550-577
Northern Zhou	557-581

Sui dynasty	581-617
Tang dynasty	618-907
Five (Northern) dynasties	907-960
Later Liang	907-922
Later Tang	923-936
Later Jin	937-948
Later Han	946-950
Later Zhou	951-960
Ten Kingdoms	902-979
Wu	902-937
Southern Tang	937-975
Wu Yue	907-978
Former Shu	903-925
Later Shu	934-965
Min	909-945
Northern Han	951-979
Southern Han	917-971
Jingnan	907-963
Chu	927-951
China Periphery	
South (Yungui macroregion)	
Nan Zhao	649-937
Dali	937-1254
North/Northwest	
Liao dynasty (Qidan)	947-1125
Xi Xa (Tangut)	1038-1227
Jin dynasty (Jurchen)	1115-1234
Song dynasty	960-1279
Northern Song	960-1127
Southern Song	1127-1279
Yuan dynasty (Mongol)	1279-1368
Ming dynasty	1368-1644
Qing dynasty (Manchu)	1644-1911
Republic of China	1912-1949
People's Republic of China	1949-present

Introduction

Symbols of Power: *Masterpieces from the Nanjing Museum* consists of more than 250 objects ranging from the Neolithic period (c. 5000 BC) through the Qing dynasty (1644-1911). More than half of the objects seen in these halls once formed part of the vast Qing imperial collections. The remaining objects have been excavated from sites in the area around Nanjing City in Jiangsu province. Although art had been collected by emperors for centuries, it was under the Qing emperor Qianlong (1736-95) that the imperial art collection grew to its largest size, both through the voracious acquisition of masterworks of the past and through production of artworks by imperial workshops and court painters. It is this collection that is the basis of some of the finest collections of Chinese art in the world, including the Palace Museum in Beijing, the Palace Museum in Taipei, and the Nanjing Museum.

The story of how the imperial collection was divided among these museums is bound up with China's turbulent modern history. The collection remained in the hands of the last emperor, Puyi, until he was turned out of Beijing's Forbidden City in 1924. In the next year, the Palace Museum was established, and for the first time, the magnificent collection was available for viewing by the general public. In 1931, the Japanese occupied Manchuria, posing a direct threat to the city of Beijing. This prompted the Nationalist government of Chiang Kai-shek to ship some 20,000 crates containing the collection first to the southern city of Shanghai and then to Nanjing. When the Japanese invaded Nanjing in 1937, the treasures were moved again. Exposed to air attacks, artillery barrages, and machine-gun fire, the convoys containing this precious cargo slowly made their way through the war zones over land and water, arriving in Sichuan province in 1939. Amazingly, most of the collection survived.

After the surrender of the Japanese on September 9, 1945, the objects were taken back to Nanjing and stored in underground bunkers at what was then called the National Central Museum. Shortly thereafter, a civil war broke out as the Communists under Mao Zedong and the Nationalists under Chiang Kai-shek fought for control of China. When Chiang Kai-shek realized that defeat was imminent in 1948, he removed a large part of the collection to Taiwan. The remaining pieces were sent to the Palace Museum in Beijing, while 2,200 crates remained in Nanjing.

The extraordinary efforts made to preserve ancient bronzes and jades, paintings, calligraphy, embroidery, and porcelain among other things, point to the legitimating power of art and ornament for rulers of China - and is the story of this exhibition. These symbols of power were produced at different times for use in different places. Therefore, the artworks in this exhibition are organized according to their physical and social context: the tomb, the temple, the court, and beyond the court, to introduce the changing uses and meanings of art and ornament throughout China's 5,000 year history.

Jade Dragon *Pei*
Western Han dynasty, (second century BC)
Length: 14.6 cm.
Excavated from the Tomb of the King of Chu at Shizishan, Xuzhou, Jiangsu province

This S-shaped dragon pendant, excavated from the tomb of the King of Chu, a vassal kingdom during the Han, is an example of jade possessed only by members of the imperial family and high-ranking members of the nobility. It is made of fine pale jade from Khotan, with an all-over "sprouting grain" design on one side and traces of carving on the other.

A copy of Matteo Ricci's "Map of the World"
Ming dynasty (1608)
Height: 182 cm; Width: 417 cm

The original Map of the World by Matteo Ricci (1552-1610), the Italian Jesuit priest who lived in China from 1583-1610, was produced over a period of eighteen years, with the final version published in 1602. Several copies of his map were also made, of which only two remain, including this version made by palace eunuchs in 1608, the 36th year of the Wanli reign (1573-1620). The names of the countries are written in Chinese phoenetic equivalents. Included in the map is Matteo Ricci's preface, explanatory notes on the various countries, as well as colophons by famous

SYMBOLS OF POWER *IN THE TOMB*

Most Neolithic objects have been excavated from burial sites. In this exhibition, the elegantly painted ceramic bowls, highly stylized wine vessel and abstract, geometric jades were excavated from sites belonging to the East Coast Neolithic cultures concentrated in the Shandong/Jiangsu/Zhejiang provinces. Their non-utilitarian shapes and decor and absence of signs of wear and tear suggest that these were ritual objects, perhaps used in offerings to gods and ancestors. The superb execution and meticulous design of these objects also tell us that these societies had a skilled and organized labor force producing objects for a powerful ruling group.

Distinctive jades, shaped into square tubes pierced with circular holes of varying lengths, and into disks, are hallmarks of the Liangzhu culture (c. 3300-2250 BC) located in the Yangzi River valley. Texts on ritual from around 300 BC identify them as *cong* and *bi*, and link them to the worship of heaven and earth, but this probably reflects the beliefs of the period in which the texts were produced rather than the beliefs of the Liangzhu people. A drill and an abrasive such as sand were used to bore the holes, grind the shapes, and carve the surfaces of these jades. It was painstaking work that required an extraordinary amount of effort. These jades have been found arranged around the bodies of male corpses, perhaps having a protective function. They were also a marker of status. In some burials, scores of these jades have been found, indicating the high rank of the deceased. The most sophisticated jades were incised with schematized animal masks comprised of two staring eyes, horns, and a grimacing mouth. On others, a human-like figure wearing a headdress appears to grapple with these ferocious creatures.

In Bronze-Age and early dynastic China, the worlds of the living and the dead were seen as a continuum, and the objects buried with the dead were believed to have the power to affect both the afterlife of the dead and the day-to-day existence of the living. Inscriptions on bronzes excavated from pit-burials of the Shang and Western Zhou periods tell us that food and wine were placed in these vessels and offered to deceased members of the ruling clan in ritual banquets. Placed on altars in temples when the royal clan member was alive, bronzes were also buried with the dead, perhaps to continue worship even after becoming ancestors themselves.

In the middle of the Eastern Zhou period (c. 770-256 BC), tombs and their contents underwent a significant change. Now, tombs were organized as horizontal multi-roomed dwellings, resembling the residences of the living. The burial objects found in these rooms reflected the function of each space and were intended to ensure the comfort, wealth, and status of the deceased in the afterlife. Tombs were also seen as doorways to the afterlife, and burial objects made of jade, bronze, and pottery took on new meanings related to early Daoist beliefs in longevity and immortality. Preserving the remains of the deceased was considered analogous to achieving immortality, and individual jade pieces have been found plugging the orifices of lower-ranking members of the elite, while emperors and princes were enshrouded in jade armour sewn together with gold or silver thread. Jade disks, first seen in the Neolithic period, were still being used in the Han dynasty, as is shown by an unusual example in this exhibition which was found affixed to the outside of a coffin with a bronze nail. In this case, the jade *bi* probably was intended to have a talismanic function: to ward off demons and other evil influences that might impede the deceased's journey to immortal paradise. Bronze mirrors, placed on or near the corpse, probably had a similar function of deflecting evil influences that might impede the soul's journey. It was also in this period that figural representation rather than ornamentation became a dominant feature of excavated artifacts and tomb decoration. The gilt-bronze ink-slab box in the form of a guardian creature is both utilitarian writing tool and guardian of the deceased. Scenes of everyday life, immortal paradise, and guardian spirits of the four directions decorate the walls of the tombs from the Han through the Tang and beyond. Images and models of houses, farms, animals, and figures of servants, entertainers, and guards were interred to make the deceased comfortable in his afterlife home. Known as *mingqi*, these "articles of the spirit" replaced the early Bronze-Age practice of burying real objects and persons. It was hoped that the malevolent spirits of the deceased could be mollified through proper ritual observance and the use of burial objects to sustain the dead's existence in the afterlife.

Bronze Deer

Warring States period (c. 450–221)

Height: 52 cm

Excavated from a Western Han tomb, Sanlidun, Lianshui, Jiangsu province, in 1965

This naturalistic bronze recumbent deer was cast in sections; the antlers and legs were cast in separate molds and then joined to the body. The deer's body, neck, and ears are inlaid with turquoise pieces. When the sculpture was excavated, the hollow body still contained the original clay core. The artisan masterfully rendered the deer's proportions and musculature and conveyed the animal's alert yet gentle nature. It is likely that the bronze mirror excavated from the same site rested on the deer's antlers.

Bronze Mirror

Warring States period (c. 450-221)

Diameter: 29 cm

Excavated from a Western Han tomb, Sanlidun, Lianshui, Jiangsu province, in 1965

The back and front of the mirror were cast separately and then joined together. The back of the mirror, which does not have the usual handle, is embellished with an interlaced hydra/snake design, with the central square of this pattern further divided into four parts by the animals' bodies. The design is inlaid with silver, and three bronze rings are attached to the mirror's periphery. Two oval jade bi are attached to one of the rings. The mirror and the bronze deer illustrated opposite were excavated from the same tomb.

Jade Shroud Sewn with Silver Wire
Eastern Han dynasty (25-220)
Length: 170 cm
Excavated from Tomb Number 1, Tushan, Xuzhou, Jiangsu province, in 1970

This jade shroud consists of twelve units, including coverings for the head and face, a pair of sleeves, gloves, trousers, and shoes. Each unit is composed of thin, celadon-colored jade pieces of varying sizes. The four corners of the individual jade pieces are pierced and sewn together with silver wire. The shroud is comprised of more than 2,600 individual pieces of jade and 800 grams of silver wire. Texts from the period tell us that only members of the nobility were buried in these jade suits; their rank was further distinguished by the use of gold, silver, or copper wire. The silver wire used here suggests that the deceased may have been a prince.

Pottery Figure of a Woman

Southern Dynasties, Liu Song period (420-479)
Height: 37.5 cm.
Excavated from a tomb at Xishanqiao, Nanjing, Jiangsu province, in 1960

This female figure was discovered in front of a coffin in the famous brick tomb decorated with scenes of the Seven Sages of the Bamboo Grove at Xishanqiao outside Nanjing. Her delicate facial features, sloping shoulders, and slender waist are physical traits associated with women from southern China. Her hair is done in an elaborate style. The tips of her feet peek out from under a long gown tied at the waist. Smiling with her hands demurely folded, her gentle demeanor suggests that she is a servant or attendant.

Pottery Warrior with Shield

Eastern Jin dynasty (317-420)
Height: 50.2 cm
Excavated at Fuguishan, Nanjing, Jiangsu province

Historical records tell us that the cemetery belonging to Eastern Jin emperors is located at Fuguishan outside Nanjing. The discovery of a stele inscribed with the words "Dark Palace of Emperor Gong" further indicates that Fuguishan is the site of an imperial burial ground. This pottery warrior, excavated not far from where the stele was discovered, was probably buried in Emperor Gong's tomb. The warrior wears a short robe with narrow sleeves and a cap. Traces of red pigment remain on the shield in his left hand. He once held a weapon in his right hand.

Molded Grey Pottery Bricks with the Animals of the Four Directions
Southern Dynasties, Eastern Jin, Longnan reign, 2nd year (398)
Length: 31.5 cm; Height: 18 cm; Width: 4.5 cm
Discovered at a farm outside Zhenjiang, Jiangsu province, in 1972

In Chinese mythology, the four directions are guarded by four mythical animals and their respective colors: a tortoise entwined by a snake known as the Black Warrior of the North, the Red Bird of the South, the Green Dragon of the East, and the White Tiger of the West. Here, these guardian animals are molded in high relief on pottery bricks that once decorated the walls of an underground tomb. The Dark Warrior brick has an inscription that reads: "This tomb was built in the second year of the Longan reign period (398), [Eastern] Jin Dynasty. Inscribed by the descendants of Yangshan. Peace and longevity for ten-thousand years."

Jade Cong

Neolithic period, Liangzhu Culture (c. 2500 BC)
Diameter: 10.2 cm
Excavated from Tomb 4, Zhangling, Wu county, Jiangsu province

Tube-shaped jades with a square cross-section and circular bore are known as *cong*. This example is unusual for its round cross-section. Worked from greenish-yellow jade, the original brown skin can be seen on one side, while the other side has a reddish hue from being underground for thousands of years. Finely incised animal masks embellish the four sides of the *cong*. Jade is a very hard stone and extremely difficult to work. An abrasive and drill must have been used to bore through it.

Jade *Bi* Disk

Western Han dynasty (first century BC)
Excavated from Tomb 2, at Mount. Shenju, Gaoyou, Jiangsu province

Perforated jade disks, known as *bi* and first seen in the Neolithic Liangzhu culture, were still being buried with deceased people as late as the Han period. Only the highest quality jade was used for burial and ritual jades. This disk was found hanging on the outside of a coffin when it was excavated from a Western Han tomb. The copper nail in the center was used to fix it to the coffin. The streaks on the surface are traces of silk bands used to hold the disk in place.

SYMBOLS OF POWER *IN THE TEMPLE*

Throughout China's long history, political and spiritual power have been inextricably linked. From the Bronze Age (Xia, Shang and Zhou dynasties), rulers were believed to have access to the spirit world and, therefore, to be deserving of supreme political power.

In the Shang (c. 1500-1050 BC) and Western Zhou (c. 1050-770 BC) periods bronze vessels and objects were the pre-eminent symbols of political power. The ruling clans derived their power from their ancestors, who were regarded as divine. From inscriptions found on some of the bronzes, we know that these vessels once contained food and wine offered to the royal ancestors in ritual banquets. One interpretation of the masks and fantastic animal imagery that decorate bronzes of this period is that they played a mediatory role in bringing together the living descendents and divine ancestors. Bronze vessels were also used as tokens of exchange between nobles, commemorating alliances, marriages, and enfeoffments. Because of the spiritual and political power associated with bronzes, the ruling clans of the Shang and Western Zhou maintained tight control over the number of bronzes produced, their iconography and style.

During the Warring States period (c. 450-221 BC) of the Eastern Zhou, fiefdoms ostensibly owing allegiance to the Zhou state competed with each other for dominance. As warlords increasingly eroded the power of the Zhou clan, ritual bronzes were diffused to a broader group. Now regional warlords had their own workshops, and bronzes with widely varying shapes, styles and iconography emerged. These vessels were fashioned into elaborate and fanciful animal shapes, and embellished with ostentatious ornament. The surfaces of the vessels were inlaid with precious materials such as turquoise, gold, and silver. Bronzes from this period are more about the naked display of power through conspicuous consumption than about sacred rites of ancestor worship. Despite the shift from sacred to secular meanings of bronzes of this period, ancestor worship has been a constant throughout China's long history, practiced by rulers and common people alike. Ancient ritual vessels first seen in Bronze Age China continued to be used in ancestor worship as late as the Qing dynasty.

Buddhism was introduced to China from India sometime in the first-second centuries BC. By the fifth century, major Buddhist monuments such as the giant Buddhas and bodhisattvas at cave-temples at Yungang and Longmen were being sponsored by imperial patrons. Sponsorship of religious monuments and deities had both devotional and ideological objectives. On the one hand, in sponsoring the production of religious objects and monuments, the imperial donor accrued merit in the next world; the more expensive the material, the more intricate and time-consuming the design, the more merit accrued by the donor. On the other, sponsorship identified the ruling house with the deity's spiritual power. In this exhibition, the gold stupa dated to the first year of the Guangxu reign (1875-1908) demonstrates this beautifully. Made of gold and ornamented with rubies and emeralds, the inscription further emphasizes its expense by recording how many grams of gold were used to make it. It also states that the stupa - a reliquary for sacred remains of holy figures - stored the hair of the previous Tongzhi emperor (1862-1874), implying his holy status.

During the Yuan (1279-1368), Ming (1368-1644) and Qing dynasties (1644-1911), Tibet was politically and strategically important to the Chinese empire. To strengthen relations, Tibetan-style Buddhism was promoted by the court. Nepalese and Tibetan religious leaders presented devotional objects to the Chinese court, introducing new media, iconography, and art styles to China, and spawning an aesthetic that melded Chinese and Tibetan styles and iconography. Most of the Buddhist statues and mandalas in this exhibition can be identified with this "Sino-Tibetan" style. In the Qing period, temples and monasteries were established throughout the empire, and shrines were established in the Forbidden City itself. Many of the objects in this exhibition, as attested to by their inscriptions, were produced by imperial workshops employing Tibetan, Mongolian, and Han Chinese artisans, and were meant for the emperor's personal devotion.

Another of China's major teachings, religious Daoism, derives its name from the Chinese character "Dao", which means "the way". It is based in part on an ancient philosophy describing the internal workings of the universe. As set forth in texts from the Warring States and Han periods, there is no supreme being, only self-generating principles like *yin* and *yang* that mutually complement and interact with one another, creating all things in the universe. By the fifth century BC, however, Daoism had become a complex religion that also incorporated beliefs in the possibility of immortality and gods and ghosts. The Daoist religion eventually included a vast pantheon of gods, celestial paradises, and underworld realms. Daoist rituals were held at court to ensure prosperity, protection, and harmony for the empire, and emperors and empresses were ordained as priests. The lacquer amulet in this exhibition carved with Daoist symbols and sacred writing, called a talisman, was used in Daoist rituals at the Ming dynasty court of the Jiajing emperor (1522-1566), a particularly ardent devotee. Invested with powers over deities in the heavenly realm, the emperor's power was justified in the human realm.

Bronze *Gong* Wine Vessel with Phoenix Pattern

Western Zhou period (c. 1050-771 BC)
Height: 21.2 cm; Length: 21.8 cm
Excavated from Yandunshan, Dantu, Jiangsu province, in 1954

This ritual vessel used for wine is one of a pair found at the Yandunshan tomb. It is fashioned into a four-legged horned animal. The lid is set into its curved back. A dragon-shaped handle is attached to the rear. The body is decorated with fantastic animal motifs such as crested birds, dragons, and elephants against a *leiwen*, or thunder-pattern, background.

**Bronze *Hu* Wine Vessel
Inlaid with Gold and Silver**

Warring States period (c. 450-221 BC)
Height: 74 cm

Hu wine vessels were used during ritual offerings to the ancestors during the Shang and Zhou periods. The circular base is supported on the outspread wings of three fantastic birds. The rim, shoulder, and neck are decorated with bands of clouds set in triangular shapes, while the belly is ornamented with lozenges inlaid with turquoise, gold, and silver. Three fledglings perch on the lid, as if ready to fly off. Another fantastic bird stands atop a five-petal plum-blossom knob in the center of the lid. It extends its neck, as if it is singing. The bird appendages, which were cast separately and then joined to the body, lighten the vessel's heavy silhouette. The complex shape and elegant decor of this wine vessel indicate the high level of skill attained by Warring States period artisans.

Carved Lacquer Sutra Box and Lid

Qing dynasty, Qianlong reign (1736-1789)
16 x 7 x 25 cm.

The inscription on the cover of the box tells us that this sutra box was made for the Qianlong reign of the great Qing dynasty. Inside, another inscription reads: "Made for Imperially-selected Buddhist scriptures". The inscription on the outside of the box is flanked by a pair of five-clawed dragons chasing a flaming pearl amongst auspicious ruyi-shaped clouds. The verso depicts the scene of Shakyamuni vanquishing demons. Seated on a throne at the top of the box, Shakyamuni's hands are in the gesture of subjugating the demons, who are being crushed beneath the throne's lotus-petal base. Altogether there are 137 figures, including the Buddha, luohans (the Buddha's disciples) and lokapalas (guardian figures), all of which are represented with different facial expressions and poses.

The Diamond Sutra (33 pages)
Qing dynasty (1644-1911)
Length: 31.3 cm; Width: 12.4 cm

This rare example of a sutra from the Qing palace is written in standard Chinese script with gold ink on indigo-dyed paper. Bordered by lotus scrolls at the top and bottom, there are illustrations of the Buddha, bodhisattvas, and the Guardians of the Four Quarters. The Guardian of Books is illustrated on the last page.

Gold Stupa for Emperor's Hair
Qing dynasty, Guangxu reign (1875-1908)
Height: 41.5 cm; Weight: 5,600 gm

Inlaid with rubies and emeralds, this stupa bears an inscription stating that it was used for storing the hair of the Tongzhi emperor (1862-1874). It also gives the date (1875) and the weight of the object as being 140 taels, or ounces (a tael being equivalent to 37.7 grams). The total of 140 taels equals 5278 grams, or about 11.1/2 pounds. A flaming gold jewel set with red coral was placed at the top of the receptacle. Chains and bells ornament the sides. The dome-shaped body resting on a square base is modeled after Tibetan-style stupas. Above the dome are thirteen steps representing the thirteen stages of enlightenment surmounted by a parasol representing heaven.

Gold Bodhisattva
Qing dynasty (1644-1911)
Height: 88 cm

A bodhisattva is a "Buddha-to-be" who has attained enlightenment but remains in the world to assist humankind. This bodhisattava stands on a lotus pedestal and wears a floral crown and jade necklace on his bare chest. His right hand points downward in a gesture of bestowing gifts. His left hand is raised in the gesture of argument, holding a lotus flower between his thumb and forefinger. This piece was produced by a Qing-dynasty imperial workshop.

Gilt-bronze Buddhist Statues
Qing dynasty, Qianlong reign (1736-1795)
Height of center piece: 20 cm

Occupying the center of this group of 50 statues is the historical Buddha, Shakyamuni. Framed by a leaf-shaped halo signifying the bodhi tree beneath which he attained enlightenment, Shakyamuni is flanked by the bodhisattvas of wisdom and compassion. In the tradition of Tibetan Buddhism, the remaining statues are organized into the five categories of spiritual beings: Buddhas, bodhisattvas, goddesses, guardians, and protectors of the Buddhist law. Most of these statues are inscribed on the base: "Respectfully made in the reign of the Qianlong Emperor of the Great Qing dynasty".

SYMBOLS OF POWER *AT COURT*

From at least the Han dynasty on, imperial workshops produced art, ornament, furnishings and regalia for the symbolically charged environment of the court, epitomized by the Forbidden City in Beijing. Built in the early years of the Ming dynasty, the complex is laid out on a north-south axis. Broad open spaces alternate with solid gates and buildings to evoke the endless alternation of the *yin-yang* cycle and cosmic harmony. As the administrative center and residence of the Son of Heaven, the Forbidden City was considered the heart of the empire, where heaven and earth met. The center of the complex is the Hall of Supreme Harmony, where the emperor conducted affairs of state, receiving officials and rulers from foreign lands. Behind the public halls of the outer court are residential and recreational areas of the inner court: offices of imperial bureaucracy, workshops, and the private temples, study, and gardens of the emperor and empress.

Public areas like the Hall of Supreme Harmony were organized into formal, symmetrical spaces intended to convey power and stability, serving as a metaphor for the ideal attributes of imperial power. Furniture, clothing, and textiles, seals and other regalia were decorated with the emblems of imperial power, such as dragons and phoenixes. The founder of the Ming, the Hongwu emperor (reign: 1368-1398) issued sumptuary laws restricting the use of imperial symbols of power like dragons and phoenixes by nobility and commoners. Only the emperor was entitled to wear clothing and possess objects emblazoned with the five-clawed dragon and twelve insignia of rulership. Though yellow was considered the pre-eminent color of the emperor, he also wore blue, red, white, or black robes during seasonal sacrifices held at temples corresponding to the four cardinal directions.

Carrying a *ruyi* scepter, the emperor would have been seated on an elaborately carved throne set on a dais. As Chinese officials and foreign rulers approached, they were expected to prostrate themselves and knock their head on the ground in a kowtow. Official court dress was also closely regulated, and from his high perch the emperor could scrutinize the supplicants. In the Qing dynasty, rank badges with emblematic animals and birds were sewn onto the robes worn by officials as clear signs of their civil and military rank. When officials received titles from the emperor, they also received objects proclaiming this honor, such as the porcelain *meiping* jar seen in this exhibition. In the Qing dynasty, the wives of officials were entitled to wear badges and headdresses related to their husbands' ranks, as is shown by two examples in this exhibition.

The private spaces of the palace were more informal and furnished with objects reflecting the scholarly curiosity and collecting habits of the emperor or empress. It was here that Qing emperors composed poetry and practiced calligraphy and ink painting, the pre-eminent arts of the literati scholar-official class. Perhaps the emperor indulged his interest in scientific developments by experimenting with the latest technological gadgets or satisfied his curiosity about foreign lands by examining a copy of the map of the world made by the Jesuit priest Matteo Ricci.

During the Ming and Qing dynasties, craft workshops under court supervision were located in Beijing and in regional centers around the empire to supply the court with the finest lacquers, porcelain, textiles, and goldwork. It is also in this period that objects were inscribed with reign dates of the dynasty in which they were made. Lacquer workers were brought to Beijing from the south to produce elaborately carved red lacquer furniture and boxes. In other cases, an imperial supervisor was sent to regional workshops, as in the case of the famous kilns at Jingdezhen in Jiangxi province. An important center for porcelain production since the eleventh century, it was located near a ready supply of the kaolin clay needed to produce porcelain. Imperially controlled kilns at Jingdezhen produced ceramics for both everyday and ceremonial use at court beginning in the Ming dynasty. In the early Ming, white glazed and underglaze copper-red wares were produced for state and funerary rituals held at court, as exemplified by the *meiping* jar mentioned earlier. Underglaze copper-red porcelain and red lacquer were especially favored in the early years of the Ming, because the color red, pronounced *zhu* in Chinese, is a homonym of the surname of the founder of the Ming ruling house, Zhu Yuanzhang (1328-1398). In the Ming-Qing periods, designs for imperial lacquers, porcelains, and textiles were supplied to the workshops by the Department of the Imperial Household at the Forbidden City and by court painters. Dragons and phoenixes, auspicious birds, and flowers such as the lotus and the peony were often combined into highly stylized intertwining designs. These patterns became emblems of power identified with the Chinese imperium until the end of the Qing dynasty in the early 20th century.

Gold Album Bestowed on Prince Zhi by the Jiaqing Emperor

Qing dynasty, Jiaqing reign (1796-1820)
Length: 22.5 cm; Width: 10.3 cm; Weight: 2,210 gm

On the sixteenth day of the ninth month of the eighteenth year of his

Gold Seal of Prince Zhi

Qing dynasty, Jiaqing reign (1796-1820)
Height: 12.13 cm; Length: 11.3 x 11.2 cm; Weight: 10km

When the Jiaqing emperor bestowed the title of Prince Zhi on his son in 1813, he also presented him with a gold seal. The seal bears the prince's title in both Chinese and Manchu scripts. Surmounting the seal is a mythical creature with the body of a tortoise and the head and tale of a dragon, one of the legendary "nine sons" of the dragon. The creature has four claws, and flames emanate from its limbs. Its body is covered with scale and "thunder" patterns. Prince Zhi succeeded his father in 1821.

Painting of Birds and Flowers by Empress Dowager Cixi (1835-1908)

Qing dynasty, Guangxu reign (1875-1908)
Length: 131.3 cm; Width: 64.8 cm

In the (1835-1908) years of the Qing dynasty, Empress Dowager Cixi dominated the court as regent. Following the example of previous Qing emperors such as Qianlong, she was also an avid patron and practitioner of the arts of ink painting and calligraphy. Signed with an honorific signature, "imperial brush", and stamped with her seals, this piece is likely to be an example of one of her many ink paintings depicting birds and flowers. However, it is possible that it was done by a "substitute brush"- that is, by an artist who executed paintings or calligraphy in the empress' name.

Imperial Calligraphy by Emperor Qianlong

Qing dynasty, Qianlong period (1736-1795)
Length: 187.5 cm; Width: 72 cm

This scroll of calligraphy by Emperor Qianlong is in the running style of handwriting. The text is a poem composed by the emperor while he was visiting Gaoyi Garden. Both the signature (the left row) and the red seal indicate that it was written by him.

Porcelain Hexagonal Vase Decorated with Underglaze Blue Dragons on a Yellow Ground

Qing dynasty, Qianlong reign (1736-1795)
Height: 57 cm

The long, slender shape of this vase is inspired by porcelain produced in the Wanli period of the Ming dynasty. However, the two openwork lug handles attached to the neck are a feature of porcelain produced during the Qianlong rein of the Qing dynasty. Produced for the Qianlong emperor's 60th birthday, the vase is decorated with a variety of imperial and longevity symbols in underglaze blue against a background of imperial yellow. Six dragons grasping a pearl containing the Chinese character for longevity *(shou)* are seen on the hexagonal belly. The shoulder and the rim are decorated with "thunder" and highly stylized *ruyi* cloud patterns. The base is decorated with plaintain leaves, thunder, and curly vine patterns. The six-character reign mark on the bottom of this elegant vase reads: "Made in the Reign of the Qianlong Emperor of the Great Qing Dynasty".

Large Plate with Flowers and Dragons

Qing Dynasty, Kangxi reign (1662-1722)
Diameter: 40.9 cm

For daily use in the inner palace, this plate is adorned with the purple and green imperial dragons. The color scheme of white, green and purple on a yellow background was developed in the Kangxi reign and was known as the "plain three-color glaze" (*susancai*). The inside is decorated with two dragons chasing a pearl, surrounded by auspicious flowers of the four seasons - peonies, lotus, plum blossoms, chrysanthemums, and roses. Other motifs include clouds and cranes. The base bears an underglaze-blue double-bordered seal of six characters: "Made in the reign of the Kangxi Emperor of the Great Qing Dynasty".

Plate with Underglaze-red Design of Flowers
Ming dynasty, Hongwu reign (1368-1398)
Top Diameter: 57.3 cm; Bottom Diameter: 35.4 cm

Red underglaze is achieved by applying copper pigments to the unglazed biscuit, which turns red during firing. The white glaze has a bluish tinge. The red glaze has bled slightly due to high temperatures in the kiln. The plate's decor is organized into three bands: the rim band is decorated with undulating vines, the inside band has entwined peonies and chrysanthemums, and the center is decorated with rocks and peonies. This plate has a heavy clay body and a large footring.

Blue-and-White Plate with Dragon and Carp Motif

Qing dynasty, Kangxi reign (1662-1722)

Height: 6.8 cm; Top diameter: 39 cm; Bottom diameter: 28.1 cm

This blue-and-white underglaze plate was used as a daily utensil in the Qing palace. In the center of the plate, a carp, seen diving into and then leaping out of the water, struggles to swim upstream as a dragon rises out of the water with fangs and claws bared. This is a scene from the well-known tale of the carp that swam up the Yellow River to reach the rapids at "Dragon Gate". If the carp could leap across these rapids, it would become a dragon. This story came to be associated with the honor, glory, and accomplishment of passing the rigorous Civil Service examinations (the entrance to the examination hall was known as the "dragon-gate") in order to become an official.

White-glazed Jar with Lotus Leaf Shaped Cover
Ming dynasty, Hongwu reign period (1368-1399)
Height: 40 cm; Top Diameter: 17.5 cm

White glazes had been perfected in the later Yuan dynasty and often showed a blueish or greenish tinge. The cover of this jar is shaped like a lotus leaf with a peduncular hold in the flared cover brim is modelled in a modulating manner. The interior of the jar is also white glazed.

White Glazed *Meiping* Wine Jar with Inscription
Ming dynasty, Hongwu reign period (1368-1399)
Height: 40 cm
Excavated from Shetian, Nanjing, Jiangsu province

This wine jar was excavated from a large well at Shetian, which lies to the east of the ruins of the old Ming palace in Nanjing. A white porcelain *jue* and bowls were found along with it. The inscription near the top of the vase reads: "Bestowed", a phrase used by Zhu Yuanzhang (1328-1398), the founder of the Ming, on granting a title to an official. We do not know who the recipient was, nor why the jar was buried in a well. Traces of spinning patterns from being thrown on a potter's wheel remain. The flared brim, slender neck, wide, rounded shoulders, and slight concavity in the right side of the body as it tapers to the foot is akin to the elegant *meiping* produced in the Yuan dynasty. While some ceramic shapes derived from other media such as bronze, gold, and glass, the *meiping* shape emerged organically from the potter's molding of the clay on the wheel. This example was probably produced in the early years of Zhu Yuanzhang's reign (1368-1398), or even before, since he had took Nanjing as early as 1356.

Imperial Engraved Porcelain Album

Qing dynasty, Qianlong reign (1736-1795)
Length: 14.5 cm; Width: 10.5 cm.

These two folio albums are comprised of 34 etched porcelain plates: volume one has eighteen plates, and volume two has sixteen. The covers of the albums are embellished with poems written in "running script" by the Qianlong emperor. The porcelain plates are mounted onto gold-paper backing. The first two plates of the first album are inscribed with the Kangxi Emperor's (1662-1772) poem "An Ode to Cotton with Preface". Below this poem are 32 seals of the emperor. The following plates include illustrations of the cultivation and production of cotton, as well as scenes from everyday life, such as nursing mothers. Poems and explanatory text by the Qianlong emperor are set opposite the illustrations. The inscriptions and illustrations were first finely incised and then filled with Chinese ink and colors. The porcelain album is based on a book outlining the standard procedures of cotton production, published under the supervision of Fang Guancheng, Governor-General of Hebei, in 1765.

Porcelain Lotus Pot with Overglaze Decoration of Autumnal Flowers
Qing dynasty, Guangxu reign (1736-1795)
Height: 44 cm

Swallows flying among Autumnal flowers such as hibiscus and chrysanthemum decorate this large pot. The white-enamel blossoms and the different shades of black enamel used to render the stems and leaves contrast dramatically with the rich turquoise ground. The composition, elegant brushwork, and layering of color were modeled after the work of the famous Qing-dynasty bird-and-flower painters, Yun Shouping (1633-1690) and Xugu (1823-1896). Made for Empress Dowager Cixi's 60th birthday, the seal of the empress is seen near the jar's rim.

Kesi Dragon Robe

Qing dynasty (1644-1911)

Length: 135 cm; Sleeve to Sleeve: 216 cm

This imperial dragon robe is made of woven silk tapestry, known as *kesi* (cut silk). *Kesi* refers to the vertical gaps between brocade patterns, allowing light through, thereby giving the impression that the patterns are carved onto the silk. The robe is lavishly decorated with five-clawed dragons and cranes cavorting amid clouds and a variety of auspicious symbols, including the Chinese character meaning "ten thousand", and the attributes of the eight Daoist Immortals. This full-length robe opens to the side and has cuffed sleeves (to protect the back of one's hands from the cold). In the Qing dynasty, dragon robes were worn by both emperors and officials at court, though the five-clawed dragon motif is generally only found on robes worn by emperors.

Carved Lacquer Box and Lid

Qing dynasty, Qianlong reign (1736-17950)

Diameter: 35.7 cm

This round wooden box was used in the palace to hold refreshments. The character for "Spring" is carved in the center of the lid. The god of longevity is carved within the roundel of the character itself. Other auspicious emblems include a pine tree signifying longlife, bats, and deer, symbols of wealth and happiness. Five-clawed dragons flank the character, and beneath it is a box containing a number of "precious things": coral, ivory, rhinocerous horns, and silver ingots, symbols of wealth and good fortune. Beams of colors radiate from the box in all directions. The four cartouches on the perimeter contain scenes from popular tales. A gold-inlaid inscription on the base reads: "Made in the Qianlong reign of the Great Qing". Inside the cover is an inscription which reads: "Precious box of longevity and Spring".

SYMBOLS OF POWER *BEYOND THE COURT*

In early China, fine ceramics, jade, lacquer, and textiles were commissioned by powerful patrons of the ruling elite. We know that independent workshops existed as early as the Han dynasty. In the Song dynasty, rapid economic growth led to the burgeoning of independent workshops and kilns producing commodities, handicrafts, and art objects for the market. Now, famous regional kilns like those in Dingzhou, Hebei produced distinctive ceramics and porcelain. While the finest examples were offered to the court as tribute, merchants made Ding ware available to buyers throughout the Chinese empire and beyond its borders. Some of the most exquisite objects in this exhibition, such as the hammered-gold plate signed by the artisan Wen Xuan, were not commissioned by an imperial patron but were available generally to those who had the means to purchase them.

Weaving and embroidery, handicrafts traditionally practiced by women, became appreciated as an art form, as attested to by the seals and inscriptions by well-known historical figures on the mountings of two examples in this exhibition. The embroidered picture of Bodhidharma crossing the river boldly combines embroidery and ink painting, establishing an art form that was to be taken up with renewed vigor in the Ming period by female members of the Gu family in Shanghai. Embroiderers of the Gu school emulated the brushwork of famous literati painters of the past with their needlework. As can be seen from a piece in this exhibition, their work is almost indistinguishable from ink painting, prompting the influential literati painter Dong Qichang (1555-1636) to remark: "Fine embroidery can exceed painting."

The Warring States bronze vessels excavated from Han-period tombs and seen in this exhibit tell us that "antiques" may have been collected as early as the Han dynasty. In the Song dynasty, collecting ancient bronzes, jades, fine ceramics, rubbings, calligraphy, and painting was a well-established pasttime of the gentleman. In Ming and Qing China, the passion for collecting antiques and other *objets d'art* reached new heights, as is indicated by a rare Song dynasty jade hair ornament found in the tomb of a high-ranking Qing official.

By the sixteenth century, people living in China were enjoying the highest standard of living on earth. Literacy was growing, trade between China's urban centers was flourishing, and contact with the West had been established. These factors led to greater social mobility and the emergence of a luxury economy. In the late Ming through the Qing period, regional workshops arose in response to this new hunger for luxury items. Available to the discerning buyer were exquisite collectibles like the beautiful gold cicada perched on a jade leaf, the colored lacquerware writing set by the famous Shen Shaoan of Fujian, and erotically charged embroidered images of beautiful ladies.

By the seventeeth century, the production of arts and crafts was market-driven, and court taste was influenced by popular taste and trends. Imperial brocades emulated textiles from Nanjing, court ladies wore embroidered garments inspired by fashions in Suzhou and Canton. Even objects produced for occasions as important as Empress Dowager Cixi's (1838-1908) birthday, such as the porcelain lotus pot decorated with designs in the manner of famous bird-and-flower painters of the day, drew inspiration from worlds beyond the court.

Embroidered Picture of Willows and Horses by the Gu Family
Ming dynasty (1368-1644)
Length: 124 cm; Width: 43 cm

The influential Ming-dynasty literati painter Dong Qichang (1555-1636) is said to have remarked: "Fine embroidery can exceed painting." Women embroiderers of the Gu family, based in Shanghai, were renowned for their ability to emulate painting techniques in embroidery. One of the most famous embroiderers of this workshop was Han Ximeng, wife of a member of the Gu family. This scene of horses being washed among willow trees is based on a work done by Han Ximeng, who, in turn, based her design on a painting by the famous literati painter Zhao Mengfu (1254-1322) of the Yuan dynasty. In this scroll, brushwork is used in combination with needlework, a technique first developed in the Song dynasty.

Embroidered Portrait of Guanyin by Guan Zhongji

Yuan dynasty (1279-1368)
Height: 104.9 cm; Width: 49.8 cm

Guan Zhongji (1262-1319) was the wife of Zhao Mengfu, a famous Yuan-dynasty artist. An accomplished painter and calligrapher, she was also extremely skilled at embroidery, as can be seen from this rare and exquisite portrait of Guanyin, the goddess of mercy. Using silk thread, Guan Zhongji masterfully evoked the calligraphic line of ink painting in rendering the bare-footed goddess' flowing garments. Guan used her own hair to embroider the Guanyin's flowing black hair. Embroidering Guanyin's image was an act of piety, made more poignant by the use of the needlewoman's own hair.

Embroidered Picture of Bodhidharma Crossing the River
Song dynasty (960-1279)
Height: 46.3 cm; Width: 30.2 cm

By the Song dynasty, embroidery had evolved from being a utilitarian craft into an artform valued by connoisseurs. This rare silk Song-dynasty scroll depicts Bodhidharma, a Buddhist monk from south India (c. sixth century), using his magical powers to cross a river. In this piece, painting and embroidery are splendidly combined: the figure of the monk is embroidered with yellow and blue silk thread against the background of a painted river landscape. This combination of embroidery and painting had a profound effect on Gu-family embroidery in the Ming period. Although this piece is not signed, the esteem in which this piece was held is indicated by the inscriptions by well-known historical figures such as Ou Dashi and Chen Benzhong.

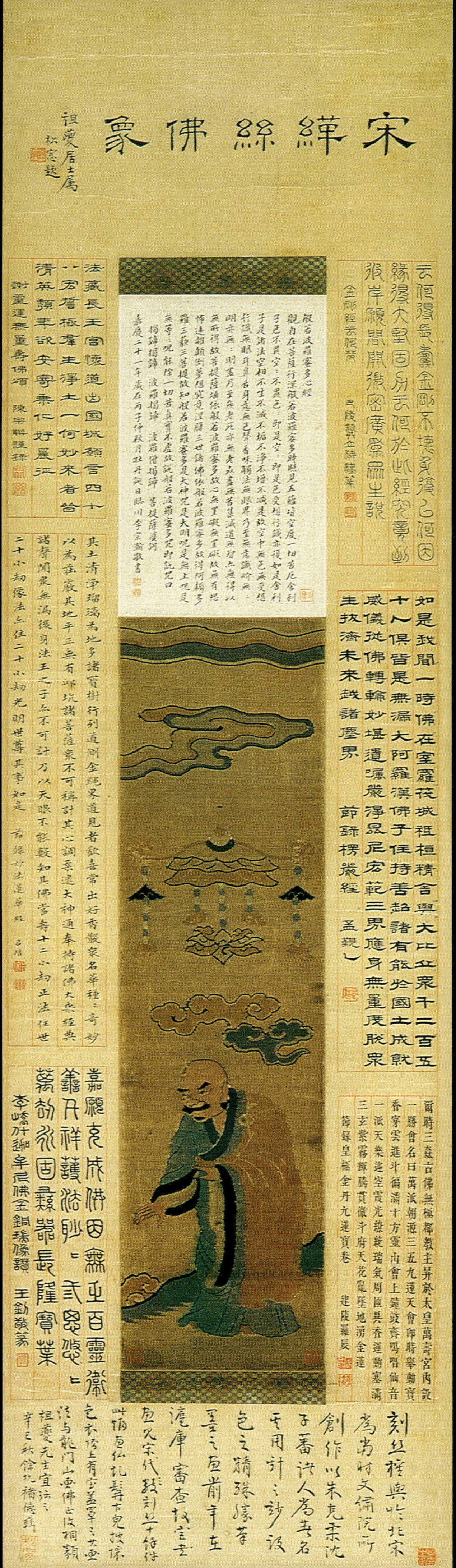

Kesi Tapestry of Buddha
Song dynasty (960-1279)
Length: 112 cm; Width: 30 cm

The *kesi* (woven silk) tapestry technique flourished in the Song dynasty, when outstanding artists produced high-quality works. This piece, depicting a Buddha figure walking beneath multicolored clouds and a canopy, represents a high point of Song woven tapestries. His gentle demeanor is conveyed by his quiet smile. Unsigned by the artist, the seals and inscriptions added by collectors on the tapestry's mounting are testament to its exquisite quality.

Gold Plate with Lotus-flower Pattern
Yuan Dynasty (1279-1368)
Length: 16 cm; Width: 16 cm
Excavated from the tomb of Lu Shimeng, Wu county, Jiangsu Province, in 1959

This exquisite plate, molded and hammered from a single piece of gold, is in the shape of four overlapping clouds. It is engraved with a variety of interlaced flowers and plants including pomegranate, lotus, crabapple, chrysanthemum, peony, and camellia, among others. Each of these flowers has auspicious connotations. For example, the pomegranate symbolizes human fertility and many offspring, and the chrysanthmum long life. The *ruyi* clouds convey the blessing "as you wish". The signature of the famous Yuan-dynasty goldsmith Wen Xuan is engraved on the bottom of the plate.

Gold Phoenix Crown

Qing dynasty, Qianlong reign (1756-1795)

Height: 15 cm.

Excavated from the tomb of Bi Yuan and his wife at Lingyanshan, Wu county, Jiangsu Province in 1970

This gold crown was excavated from the tomb of Bi Yuan (1730-1797), a famous Qing official and scholar, and his wife. The gold wire frame is decorated with birds, flowers, seven phoenixes among the clouds and two dragons in pursuit a flaming pearl. On the periphery of the crown are medallions inscribed with the characters: *yue* (moon), *tian* (heaven), *feng* (bestow), and *ri* (sun). In the center top of the crown is a plaque inscribed with the words "*en rong*". In the middle of the crown are medallions with characters *gao*, *ming*, *chao*, and *guan*. Taken together, these characters indicate that this crown was bestowed upon Bi Yuan's wife when he received an honorific rank by imperial decree.

Gold Cicada on a Jade Leaf

Ming dynasty (1368-1644)

Length: 5.3 cm

Excavated from the Wufengshan site, Wu county, Jiangsu province, in 1954

A life-like cicada made of 24-karat gold rests on a finely incised leaf of flawless, pure white jade from Khotan. This masterpiece is by an unknown but obviously gifted artisan of the Jiangnan region in the Ming dynasty. Gold and jade together represent prosperity, and the cicada is a symbol of continuous life. The solid-gold cicada enhances the delicate, almost translucent quality of the jade. Excavated from a Ming-dynasty tomb in Wu county in Jiangsu province, it was discovered lying next to the head of a woman and is believed to be a hair ornament.